TABLE OF CONTENTS

Introduction:
- Welcome to the world of insurance sales.
- Importance of insurance producers in the industry.
- Overview of what to expect from the book.

Chapter 1: Understanding the Insurance Industry
- Overview of the insurance industry.
- Types of insurance (life, health, property, casualty, etc.).
- Key players and stakeholders.

Chapter 2: Developing a Solid Foundation
- Understanding the basics of insurance terminology.
- Familiarizing yourself with common policies and coverage types.
- Learning about regulatory requirements and compliance.

Chapter 3: Mastering Sales Techniques
- Effective communication skills.
- Building rapport with clients.
- Understanding customer needs and tailoring solutions.

Chapter 4: Prospecting and Lead Generation
- Identifying target markets.
- Utilizing various prospecting methods (cold calling, networking, referrals, etc.).
- Leveraging technology for lead generation.

Chapter 5: Conducting Needs Assessments
- Importance of thorough needs assessments.
- Asking the right questions to uncover client needs.
- Using needs assessments to tailor insurance solutions.

Chapter 6: Presenting Solutions and Overcoming Objections
- Crafting compelling proposals.
- Addressing common objections.
- Techniques for closing the sale.

Chapter 7: Building and Managing Client Relationships
- Importance of customer retention.
- Providing exceptional customer service.
- Strategies for staying in touch with clients.

Chapter 8: Leveraging Technology and Tools
- Utilizing CRM systems for managing leads and clients.
- Automation tools for streamlining processes.
- Online resources for continued learning and development.

Chapter 9: Navigating Regulations and Compliance
- Staying up-to-date with industry regulations.
- Importance of ethical conduct.
- Mitigating compliance risks.

Chapter 10: Continuous Learning and Improvement
- Importance of ongoing education and training.
- Seeking mentorship and guidance.
- Setting goals and measuring success.

Conclusion:
- Recap of key takeaways.
- Encouragement to apply knowledge and take action.
- Wishing success in their journey as an insurance producer.

INTRODUCTION

Welcome to the thrilling world of insurance sales! As you embark on this journey, allow me, a seasoned insurance producer who has traversed the highs and lows of this dynamic industry, to extend my heartfelt congratulations. You've chosen a path that demands resilience, ingenuity, and a relentless pursuit of excellence. But fear not, for within these pages lies a roadmap to guide you towards unparalleled success.

Having spent years honing my craft at a prestigious firm, I understand the exhilarating highs of closing a deal and the daunting challenges that accompany the pursuit of mastery in this field. Each day presents a new opportunity to impact lives, to safeguard dreams, and to forge lasting relationships with clients. Yet, success in insurance sales is not merely measured by revenue figures or accolades but by the profound difference we make in the lives of those we serve.

In this playbook, you will find a wealth of knowledge distilled from years of experience, from the fundamentals of insurance principles to the intricacies of sales psychology. Whether you're a fresh-faced novice eager to carve your niche or a seasoned professional seeking to refine your approach, this guide is tailored to equip you with the tools, strategies, and insights necessary to thrive in the competitive landscape of insurance sales.

But let me be clear: success in this industry is not guaranteed, nor is it easily attained. It requires dedication, perseverance, and an unwavering commitment to continuous improvement. Yet, with the right mindset and a willingness to embrace challenges as opportunities for growth, the sky is truly the limit.

So, as you embark on this exhilarating journey, I urge you to approach each day with a sense of purpose, passion, and unwavering determination. Remember, the road to success may be fraught with obstacles, but with the right guidance and perseverance, you have the power to achieve greatness.

Welcome to the ranks of insurance producers, where every interaction is an opportunity to make a difference, and every challenge is a stepping stone towards success. Embrace the journey, and may this playbook serve as your trusted companion as you navigate the exhilarating world of insurance sales.

CHAPTER 1

Understanding the Insurance Industry

Welcome to the dynamic and multifaceted world of the insurance industry! In this chapter, we'll embark on a journey to understand the fundamental principles, structures, and dynamics that shape the insurance landscape.

1.1 Overview of the Insurance Industry:
- Definition of insurance and its role in risk management.
- Historical evolution of the insurance industry.
- The significance of insurance in modern society.

1.2 Types of Insurance:
- Life Insurance: Providing financial protection to beneficiaries in the event of the insured's death.
- Health Insurance: Covering medical expenses and promoting wellness.
- Property Insurance: Protecting against damage or loss of property due to unforeseen events.
- Casualty Insurance: Providing liability coverage for accidents and injuries.
- Specialty Lines: Exploring niche insurance products tailored to specific industries or risks.

1.3 Key Players and Stakeholders:
- Insurance Companies: Underwriters of insurance policies and providers of financial protection.
- Insurance Agents and Brokers: Intermediaries who facilitate transactions between insurance companies and clients.
- Regulatory Bodies: Government agencies responsible for overseeing the insurance industry and ensuring compliance with laws and regulations.
- Consumers: Individuals and businesses seeking protection against various risks.
- Reinsurers: Companies that provide insurance to insurance companies, spreading risk and ensuring solvency.

1.4 Trends and Innovations:
- Technological Advancements: The impact of artificial intelligence, big data analytics, and digital platforms on insurance operations.
- Shifts in Consumer Behavior: Changing preferences and expectations of insurance buyers.
- Regulatory Changes: Updates to laws and regulations governing the insurance industry.
- Emerging Risks: Addressing new and evolving risks such as cyber threats, climate change, and pandemics.

1.5 Career Opportunities in Insurance:
- Insurance Producer: Roles and responsibilities of insurance agents and brokers.
- Claims Adjuster: Investigating and settling insurance claims.
- Underwriter: Assessing risk and determining insurance premiums.
- Risk Manager: Identifying and managing risks for individuals and organizations.
- Actuary: Analyzing data to assess risk and calculate insurance premiums.

1.6 Conclusion:
- Recap of key concepts discussed in this chapter.
- Importance of understanding the fundamentals of the insurance industry.
- Excitement for the journey ahead as we delve deeper into the world of insurance sales and service.

In the next chapter, we'll explore the foundational knowledge and skills necessary to thrive as an insurance producer. Stay tuned as we embark on this rewarding and fulfilling journey together!

CHAPTER 2

Developing a Solid Foundation

In this chapter, we'll lay the groundwork for your journey towards becoming a successful insurance producer. Building a solid foundation of knowledge and understanding is crucial for navigating the complexities of the insurance industry with confidence and competence.

2.1 Understanding the Basics:
- Terminology: Familiarize yourself with key insurance terms such as premium, deductible, coverage limits, and exclusions.
- Policy Components: Learn about the various elements of an insurance policy, including declarations, insuring agreements, conditions, and endorsements.
- Claims Process: Gain insight into how insurance claims are filed, processed, and settled, including the roles of policyholders, insurers, and claims adjusters.

2.2 Familiarizing Yourself with Common Policies:
- Life Insurance: Explore the different types of life insurance policies, such as term life, whole life, and universal life, and understand their features, benefits, and suitability for different client needs.

- Health Insurance: Learn about the components of health insurance plans, including premiums, copayments, deductibles, and coverage for medical services, prescription drugs, and preventive care.
- Property and Casualty Insurance: Understand the coverage provided by property and casualty insurance policies, including protection against damage or loss to homes, vehicles, businesses, and personal belongings.

2.3 Learning About Regulatory Requirements and Compliance:
- State Regulations: Familiarize yourself with the insurance laws and regulations specific to the state(s) in which you operate, including licensing requirements, continuing education obligations, and consumer protection provisions.
- Ethical Standards: Understand the ethical considerations and professional standards that govern the conduct of insurance producers, including honesty, integrity, confidentiality, and disclosure of conflicts of interest.
- Compliance Practices: Develop an awareness of compliance best practices, including record-keeping requirements, advertising guidelines, and disclosure obligations to clients.

2.4 Professional Development Opportunities:
- Continuing Education: Stay abreast of industry developments and regulatory changes through ongoing education and training programs offered by insurance associations, professional organizations, and accredited institutions.
- Networking Events: Participate in industry conferences, seminars, and networking events to connect with fellow insurance professionals, exchange knowledge and insights, and stay informed about emerging trends and opportunities.
- Mentorship Programs: Seek guidance and mentorship from experienced insurance producers who can offer valuable advice, support, and encouragement as you navigate your career path in the insurance industry.

2.5 Conclusion:
- Recap of key concepts discussed in this chapter.
- Importance of building a solid foundation of knowledge and understanding in the insurance industry.
- Excitement for the journey ahead as you continue to expand your expertise and skills as an insurance producer.

In the next chapter, we'll delve into the art and science of mastering sales techniques to effectively engage with clients, address their needs, and deliver value through insurance solutions. Get ready to unleash your potential and elevate your sales game to new heights!

CHAPTER 3

Mastering Sales Techniques

In this chapter, we'll explore the art and science of mastering sales techniques that are essential for success as an insurance producer. From effective communication skills to understanding client needs and closing deals, honing your sales acumen will empower you to build meaningful relationships with clients and drive business growth.

3.1 Effective Communication Skills:
- Active Listening: Cultivate the habit of listening attentively to clients to understand their concerns, preferences, and priorities.
- Empathy: Demonstrate empathy and understanding towards clients' needs and challenges to build trust and rapport.
- Clear and Concise Communication: Communicate complex insurance concepts in simple and easy-to-understand language to ensure clarity and comprehension.
- Confidence: Project confidence and professionalism in your interactions with clients to inspire trust and credibility.

3.2 Building Rapport with Clients:

- **Establishing Trust:** Build trust with clients by demonstrating integrity, reliability, and a commitment to their best interests.
- **Personalization:** Tailor your approach to each client based on their unique needs, preferences, and circumstances.
- **Authenticity:** Be genuine and authentic in your interactions with clients to foster genuine connections and long-term relationships.
- **Follow-up:** Follow up with clients regularly to maintain communication, address any concerns, and provide ongoing support and assistance.

3.3 Understanding Client Needs:

- **Needs Assessment:** Conduct thorough needs assessments to identify clients' insurance needs, goals, and risk tolerance.
- **Asking the Right Questions:** Ask open-ended questions to encourage clients to share their concerns, priorities, and objectives.
- **Identifying Pain Points:** Identify and address clients' pain points and challenges to offer relevant and personalized insurance solutions.
- **Educating Clients:** Educate clients about the importance of insurance protection and the value of the products and services you offer.

3.4 Tailoring Solutions to Client Needs:
- **Customization:** Customize insurance solutions to meet the specific needs and preferences of each client.
- **Value Proposition:** Clearly articulate the value proposition of your insurance products and services to demonstrate their benefits and advantages.
- **Comparison:** Provide clients with multiple options and help them compare different insurance products to make informed decisions.
- **Addressing Objections:** Anticipate and address clients' objections and concerns with empathy, reassurance, and factual information.

3.5 Closing the Sale:
- **Asking for the Sale:** Confidently ask clients for their business and guide them through the purchasing process.
- **Overcoming Objections:** Address any remaining objections or concerns raised by clients with empathy and professionalism.
- **Providing Assurance:** Provide clients with reassurance and support throughout the closing process to alleviate any doubts or hesitations.
- **Confirming Next Steps:** Confirm the details of the sale, outline next steps, and follow up promptly to ensure a smooth transition and onboarding process.

3.6 Conclusion:
- Recap of key concepts discussed in this chapter.
- Importance of mastering sales techniques to effectively engage with clients and drive business growth.
- Excitement for the opportunity to apply these techniques in real-world scenarios and achieve success as an insurance producer.

In the next chapter, we'll explore strategies for prospecting and lead generation to expand your client base and grow your insurance business. Get ready to uncover new opportunities and unlock your potential as a top-performing insurance producer!

CHAPTER 4
Prospecting and Lead Generation

In this chapter, we'll dive into the strategies and techniques for prospecting and lead generation that are essential for expanding your client base and growing your insurance business.

4.1 Identifying Target Markets:
- Define Your Ideal Client Profile: Identify the characteristics and demographics of your ideal clients, including age, income level, occupation, and lifestyle.
- Market Research: Conduct market research to identify potential target markets with a high demand for insurance products and services.
- Analyze Competition: Evaluate your competitors and their target markets to identify opportunities for differentiation and competitive advantage.

4.2 Prospecting Methods:
- Cold Calling: Reach out to potential clients via phone calls to introduce yourself, your services, and the benefits of insurance protection.
- Networking: Attend industry events, networking functions, and community gatherings to meet potential clients and referral partners.

- Referrals: Leverage your existing client base and professional network to ask for referrals and recommendations.
- Digital Marketing: Utilize online channels such as social media, email marketing, and content marketing to attract and engage with potential clients.

4.3 Leveraging Technology for Lead Generation:
- Customer Relationship Management (CRM) Systems: Utilize CRM systems to organize and manage your leads, track interactions, and nurture relationships with potential clients.
- Marketing Automation Tools: Implement marketing automation tools to streamline lead generation processes, automate follow-up communications, and track campaign performance.
- Website and Online Presence: Optimize your website and online presence to attract organic traffic, capture leads, and showcase your expertise and offerings.

4.4 Follow-up and Relationship Building:
- Timely Follow-up: Follow up promptly with leads to maintain momentum and demonstrate your commitment to addressing their needs.
- Personalized Communication: Personalize your follow-up communication based on the interests and preferences of each lead to build rapport and trust.

- Provide Value: Offer valuable information, insights, and resources to leads to demonstrate your expertise and establish yourself as a trusted advisor.
- Stay Connected: Stay connected with leads through regular communication, updates, and relevant content to keep them engaged and informed.

4.5 Measurement and Optimization:
- Track Key Metrics: Monitor key metrics such as lead conversion rates, pipeline velocity, and return on investment (ROI) to evaluate the effectiveness of your lead generation efforts.
- A/B Testing: Experiment with different prospecting methods, messaging, and channels to identify what resonates most with your target audience and optimize your approach accordingly.
- Continuous Improvement: Continuously review and refine your lead generation strategies based on data and insights to maximize your results and drive business growth.

4.6 Conclusion:
- Recap of key concepts discussed in this chapter.
- Importance of prospecting and lead generation in expanding your client base and growing your insurance business.
- Excitement for the opportunity to implement these strategies and techniques to attract and engage with potential clients.

CHAPTER 5
Conducting Needs Assessments

In this chapter, we'll explore the importance of conducting thorough needs assessments to understand clients' insurance needs, goals, and preferences, and tailor insurance solutions to meet their specific requirements.

5.1 Importance of Needs Assessments:
- Understand Client Needs: Gain insight into clients' financial situation, risk tolerance, and insurance objectives to recommend suitable insurance solutions.
- Build Trust and Rapport: Demonstrate your commitment to understanding and addressing clients' needs to build trust, rapport, and credibility.
- Offer Personalized Solutions: Tailor insurance solutions to match clients' unique requirements, preferences, and circumstances to provide maximum value and protection.

5.2 Asking the Right Questions:
- Open-Ended Questions: Ask open-ended questions to encourage clients to share their concerns, priorities, and objectives freely.
- Active Listening: Listen attentively to clients' responses, ask clarifying questions, and seek deeper insights to fully understand their needs and goals.

- Empathetic Approach: Show empathy and understanding towards clients' concerns and challenges to create a supportive and collaborative environment.

5.3 Comprehensive Assessment Areas:
- Financial Situation: Assess clients' income, assets, liabilities, and expenses to determine their financial stability and insurance needs.
- Risk Exposure: Identify potential risks and liabilities that clients may face, such as health issues, property damage, liability claims, or loss of income.
- Coverage Gaps: Identify any existing insurance coverage gaps or deficiencies that may leave clients vulnerable to financial loss or hardship.
- Future Goals: Discuss clients' short-term and long-term goals, such as retirement planning, wealth accumulation, or legacy planning, and explore how insurance can support their objectives.

5.4 Analyzing Needs and Prioritizing Solutions:
- Evaluate Coverage Options: Present clients with different insurance coverage options and explain the benefits, features, and costs associated with each.
- Prioritize Solutions: Prioritize insurance solutions based on clients' needs, goals, and budget constraints, and recommend appropriate coverage levels and policy features.

- Provide Recommendations: Offer recommendations and guidance on the most suitable insurance products and strategies to address clients' needs and protect their financial interests.

5.5 Documenting and Reviewing Needs Assessments:
- Documentation: Document the findings of the needs assessment process, including clients' goals, concerns, and recommended insurance solutions, in written form for reference and review.
- Review and Update: Periodically review and update clients' needs assessments to reflect changes in their circumstances, goals, or risk exposures, and adjust insurance solutions accordingly.

5.6 Conclusion:
- Recap of key concepts discussed in this chapter.
- Importance of conducting thorough needs assessments to understand clients' insurance needs and recommend appropriate solutions.
- Excitement for the opportunity to apply these principles and techniques to serve clients effectively and provide value through insurance protection.

CHAPTER 6

Presenting Solutions and Overcoming Objections

In this chapter, we'll explore the art of presenting insurance solutions effectively and overcoming objections to close sales and help clients secure the protection they need.

6.1 Crafting Compelling Proposals:
- Clear and Concise Presentation: Present insurance solutions in a clear, concise, and easy-to-understand manner to ensure clients comprehend the benefits and features.
- Highlighting Value Proposition: Emphasize the value proposition of insurance products, including financial protection, peace of mind, and long-term security, to resonate with clients' needs and priorities.
- Visual Aids: Utilize visual aids such as charts, graphs, and illustrations to illustrate complex concepts and reinforce key selling points effectively.

6.2 Addressing Common Objections:
- Price Objections: Anticipate objections related to pricing and justify the cost of insurance coverage by highlighting the long-term benefits and protection it provides.

- Coverage Concerns: Address concerns about coverage adequacy and reassure clients by explaining policy features, limits, and exclusions clearly and transparently.
- Trust and Credibility: Build trust and credibility by providing evidence of the insurer's financial strength, reputation, and track record of claims payment.
- Competition Comparison: Differentiate your offerings from competitors by highlighting unique features, benefits, and value-added services that set your insurance solutions apart.

6.3 Techniques for Closing the Sale:
- Trial Close: Gauge clients' readiness to move forward by asking trial close questions to assess their level of interest and commitment.
- Assumptive Close: Assume the sale by presenting the paperwork or discussing next steps confidently and naturally to encourage clients to take action.
- Alternative Close: Offer clients multiple options or alternatives to choose from to give them a sense of control and ownership over the decision-making process.
- Urgency and Scarcity: Create a sense of urgency and scarcity by emphasizing time-sensitive offers, limited-time promotions, or impending policy changes to motivate clients to act quickly.

6.4 Providing Assurance and Support:
- Clarifying Terms and Conditions: Review the terms and conditions of insurance policies with clients to ensure they understand their rights, obligations, and coverage provisions fully.
- Addressing Concerns: Address any remaining concerns or questions raised by clients with empathy, patience, and professionalism to alleviate doubts and build confidence.
- Offering Post-Sale Support: Provide ongoing support and assistance to clients after the sale, including policy servicing, claims assistance, and proactive communication to reinforce the value of their insurance coverage.

6.5 Conclusion:
- Recap of key concepts discussed in this chapter.
- Importance of presenting insurance solutions effectively and overcoming objections to close sales successfully.
- Excitement for the opportunity to apply these techniques and strategies to help clients secure the protection they need and achieve their financial goals.

CHAPTER 7
Building and Managing Client Relationships

In this chapter, we'll explore strategies for building and managing client relationships effectively to foster loyalty, satisfaction, and long-term retention.

7.1 Importance of Client Relationships:
- Relationship-Centric Approach: Adopt a relationship-centric approach to insurance sales and service focused on building trust, rapport, and mutual respect with clients.
- Client Lifetime Value: Recognize the long-term value of client relationships in generating repeat business, referrals, and positive word-of-mouth marketing.
- Client Advocacy: Cultivate loyal clients who become advocates for your business and ambassadors for your brand, promoting your services to their networks and communities.

7.2 Providing Exceptional Customer Service:
- Responsive Communication: Respond promptly to client inquiries, requests, and concerns to demonstrate your commitment to providing timely and attentive service.
- Proactive Outreach: Initiate proactive outreach to clients to check in on their satisfaction, provide updates, and offer assistance or guidance as needed.

- Personalized Attention: Tailor your interactions and communications to each client's preferences, interests, and communication style to create a personalized and memorable experience.

7.3 Strategies for Staying in Touch:
- Regular Communication: Stay in touch with clients through regular communication channels such as phone calls, emails, newsletters, and social media to maintain engagement and top-of-mind awareness.
- Value-Added Content: Share valuable information, resources, and insights with clients on topics relevant to their interests, needs, and concerns to provide ongoing value and support.
- Special Events and Promotions: Host special events, webinars, or promotions exclusively for clients to express appreciation, foster camaraderie, and strengthen client relationships.

7.4 Handling Client Feedback and Concerns:
- Open Communication: Encourage open and honest communication with clients, welcome feedback and suggestions, and address any concerns or issues promptly and professionally.
- Problem Resolution: Take ownership of client issues or complaints, investigate the root cause, and proactively work towards finding a satisfactory resolution to restore trust and satisfaction.
- Continuous Improvement: Use client feedback and insights to identify areas for improvement, refine your processes, and enhance the overall client experience over time.

7.5 Navigating Challenging Situations:
- Empathy and Understanding: Show empathy and understanding towards clients facing difficult circumstances such as claims, losses, or life events, and offer support and assistance to alleviate their stress and concerns.
- Transparency and Integrity: Maintain transparency and integrity in your dealings with clients, provide honest and accurate information, and uphold your ethical and professional standards at all times.
- Turning Challenges into Opportunities: View challenging situations as opportunities to demonstrate your commitment to clients, strengthen relationships, and showcase your value as a trusted advisor and advocate.

7.6 Conclusion:
- Recap of key concepts discussed in this chapter.
- Importance of building and managing client relationships effectively to foster loyalty, satisfaction, and long-term retention.
- Excitement for the opportunity to apply these strategies and techniques to cultivate lasting and mutually beneficial relationships with clients.

CHAPTER 8
Leveraging Technology and Tools

In this chapter, we'll explore the various technology tools and resources available to insurance producers to streamline operations, enhance productivity, and deliver exceptional service to clients.

8.1 Customer Relationship Management (CRM) Systems:
- Overview: Understand the benefits and functionalities of CRM systems for organizing, managing, and tracking client interactions, leads, and opportunities.
- Lead Management: Use CRM systems to capture and track leads, record contact information, and log interactions to streamline lead management processes and improve follow-up.
- Client Communication: Utilize CRM systems to schedule follow-up tasks, send automated email campaigns, and maintain regular communication with clients to stay top-of-mind and foster engagement.

8.2 Marketing Automation Tools:
- Email Marketing Platforms: Leverage email marketing platforms to create and send targeted email campaigns, newsletters, and updates to clients and prospects to nurture relationships and generate leads.

- Social Media Management Tools: Use social media management tools to schedule posts, monitor engagement, and analyze performance metrics across multiple social media platforms to enhance your online presence and brand visibility.
- Content Management Systems (CMS): Utilize CMS platforms to create and publish content such as blog posts, articles, and resources on your website to attract organic traffic, establish thought leadership, and provide value to visitors.

8.3 Online Quoting and Proposal Generation Tools:
- Quoting Software: Explore online quoting tools and software platforms that enable you to generate insurance quotes quickly, accurately, and efficiently for clients, streamline the application process, and expedite policy issuance.
- Proposal Builders: Use proposal building tools to create professional and customized insurance proposals and presentations for clients, incorporating relevant information, visuals, and pricing details to effectively communicate the value of your offerings.

8.4 Document Management Systems:
- Document Storage: Store and organize client documents, policies, and records securely in electronic document management systems to facilitate easy access, retrieval, and sharing of information internally and with clients as needed.

- E-Signature Solutions: Implement e-signature solutions to streamline the signing and processing of insurance documents and applications digitally, reducing paperwork, minimizing errors, and accelerating transaction turnaround times.

8.5 Mobile Apps and Digital Platforms:
- Mobile Apps: Download and use mobile apps developed by insurance carriers, agencies, or third-party providers to access policy information, submit claims, request assistance, and communicate with clients on the go from your smartphone or tablet.
- Digital Platforms: Explore digital platforms and online marketplaces that offer insurance products and services directly to consumers, leveraging technology to reach new audiences, simplify purchasing, and enhance customer experiences.

8.6 Continuing Education and Training Resources:
- Online Learning Platforms: Enroll in online courses, webinars, and training programs offered by insurance associations, professional organizations, and educational institutions to expand your knowledge, develop new skills, and stay updated on industry trends and regulations.
- Virtual Workshops and Events: Participate in virtual workshops, conferences, and industry events hosted online to connect with peers, engage with experts, and exchange insights and best practices without geographical constraints.

8.7 Data Analytics and Reporting Tools:
- Analytical Tools: Utilize data analytics and reporting tools to analyze client data, track key performance indicators (KPIs), and gain insights into client behaviors, preferences, and trends to inform strategic decision-making and marketing initiatives.
- Performance Dashboards: Access performance dashboards and dashboards provided by insurance carriers, agencies, or third-party vendors to monitor sales metrics, track goals, and measure progress towards targets in real-time.

8.8 Compliance and Security Solutions:
- Compliance Management Software: Invest in compliance management software to streamline compliance processes, track regulatory requirements, and ensure adherence to industry standards and best practices.
- Data Security Measures: Implement robust data security measures and protocols to protect sensitive client information, prevent unauthorized access, and mitigate the risk of data breaches or cyberattacks.

8.9 Conclusion:
- Recap of key concepts discussed in this chapter.
- Importance of leveraging technology and tools to streamline operations, enhance productivity, and deliver exceptional service to clients.
- Excitement for the opportunity to explore and adopt innovative technologies and solutions to drive business growth and success in the insurance industry.

CHAPTER 9
Navigating Regulations and Compliance

In this chapter, we'll explore the regulatory landscape governing the insurance industry and provide guidance on navigating compliance requirements effectively to ensure ethical conduct and mitigate risks.

9.1 Overview of Regulatory Framework:
- State vs. Federal Regulation: Understand the division of regulatory authority between state and federal governments and the implications for insurance licensing, oversight, and enforcement.
- State Insurance Departments: Familiarize yourself with the roles and responsibilities of state insurance departments in regulating insurance companies, producers, and insurance products within their jurisdictions.

9.2 Licensing and Certification Requirements:
- Pre-Licensing Education: Complete pre-licensing education requirements mandated by state insurance departments, including coursework, exams, and background checks, to qualify for insurance producer licensing.
- Continuing Education: Fulfill continuing education obligations to maintain insurance producer licenses, stay updated on industry developments, and comply with regulatory requirements for license renewal.

9.3 Ethical Standards and Professional Conduct:
- Industry Codes of Ethics: Adhere to industry codes of ethics and professional standards established by insurance associations, professional organizations, and regulatory bodies to uphold principles of integrity, honesty, and fairness in your interactions with clients, colleagues, and the public.
- Fiduciary Duty: Recognize and fulfill your fiduciary duty to act in the best interests of clients, provide suitable recommendations, disclose conflicts of interest, and prioritize clients' financial well-being over your own interests or incentives.

9.4 Advertising and Marketing Compliance:
- Truthful and Non-Misleading: Ensure that advertising and marketing materials are truthful, accurate, and non-misleading, and comply with regulatory requirements for disclosing material terms, conditions, and limitations associated with insurance products and services.
- Prohibited Practices: Avoid prohibited practices such as false or deceptive advertising, bait-and-switch tactics, unfair discrimination, and unauthorized use of trademarks or endorsements that could violate consumer protection laws or regulatory standards.

9.5 Privacy and Data Security:
- Confidentiality Obligations: Safeguard the confidentiality and privacy of client information by implementing appropriate security measures, encryption protocols, and data access controls to protect against unauthorized disclosure or misuse.

- Compliance with Privacy Laws: Comply with federal and state privacy laws, such as the Health Insurance Portability and Accountability Act (HIPAA) and the Gramm-Leach-Bliley Act (GLBA), governing the collection, use, and disclosure of personal and financial information in the insurance industry.

9.6 Anti-Fraud Measures:
- Fraud Prevention: Implement anti-fraud measures and procedures to detect, deter, and prevent insurance fraud, including fraudulent claims, misrepresentation, forgery, and identity theft, to protect insurers, policyholders, and the integrity of the insurance system.
- Reporting Requirements: Report suspected instances of insurance fraud to appropriate authorities, such as state insurance departments, law enforcement agencies, or fraud bureaus, in accordance with regulatory guidelines and reporting obligations.

9.7 Record-Keeping and Documentation:
- Retention Policies: Establish record-keeping and documentation policies to maintain accurate, complete, and up-to-date records of client transactions, communications, policies, and agreements for regulatory compliance, audit purposes, and dispute resolution.
- Electronic Records: Embrace electronic record-keeping technologies and systems to digitize and archive client documents, contracts, and correspondence securely, reduce paperwork, and facilitate efficient retrieval and storage of records.

9.8 Regulatory Updates and Compliance Resources:
- Stay Informed: Stay informed about regulatory updates, changes, and developments impacting the insurance industry by subscribing to newsletters, bulletins, and updates from state insurance departments, industry associations, and regulatory agencies.
- Compliance Resources: Access compliance resources, guides, manuals, and training materials provided by insurance associations, regulatory bodies, and professional organizations to navigate regulatory requirements effectively and ensure compliance with industry standards and best practices.

9.9 Conclusion:
- Recap of key concepts discussed in this chapter.
- Importance of navigating regulations and compliance requirements effectively to ensure ethical conduct, mitigate risks, and maintain regulatory compliance in the insurance industry.
- Excitement for the opportunity to uphold high ethical and professional standards, protect consumers' interests, and contribute to the integrity and stability of the insurance marketplace.

CHAPTER 10
Continuous Learning and Improvement

In this chapter, we'll explore the importance of continuous learning and professional development in the insurance industry and provide guidance on strategies for enhancing your knowledge, skills, and expertise throughout your career.

10.1 Lifelong Learning Mindset:
- Commitment to Growth: Embrace a growth mindset and a commitment to continuous learning, improvement, and adaptation to keep pace with industry developments, technological advancements, and evolving consumer preferences.
- Intellectual Curiosity: Cultivate intellectual curiosity and a thirst for knowledge by seeking out new ideas, perspectives, and insights from diverse sources, experiences, and disciplines relevant to the insurance profession.

10.2 Ongoing Education and Training:
- Professional Designations: Pursue professional designations, certifications, and credentials offered by insurance associations, industry organizations, and educational institutions to deepen your expertise, enhance your credibility, and demonstrate your commitment to excellence.

- Continuing Education: Engage in continuing education and training programs, workshops, seminars, and webinars to stay updated on industry trends, regulatory changes, emerging risks, and best practices in insurance sales, service, and operations.

10.3 Mentorship and Coaching:
- Seek Mentorship: Seek guidance, mentorship, and coaching from experienced insurance professionals, industry leaders, or mentors within your organization to benefit from their wisdom, insights, and advice on navigating challenges, seizing opportunities, and advancing your career.
- Be a Mentor: Pay it forward by serving as a mentor or coach to aspiring insurance professionals, newcomers to the industry, or colleagues seeking guidance, support, and mentorship in their professional development journey.

10.4 Networking and Collaboration:
- Professional Associations: Join insurance associations, industry networks, and professional organizations to expand your network, connect with peers, share knowledge, and collaborate on initiatives to advance the interests of the insurance profession.
- Peer Learning Communities: Participate in peer learning communities, discussion forums, or study groups with fellow insurance professionals to exchange ideas, share experiences, and learn from each other's successes and challenges.

10.5 Thought Leadership and Industry Involvement:
- Thought Leadership: Establish yourself as a thought leader and subject matter expert in your niche or specialization within the insurance industry by publishing articles, speaking at conferences, contributing to industry publications, and sharing insights through thought leadership platforms.
- Industry Involvement: Get involved in industry committees, task forces, or advisory boards to contribute your expertise, influence policy decisions, and shape the direction of the insurance profession through active participation in industry initiatives and advocacy efforts.

10.6 Feedback and Reflection:
- Solicit Feedback: Seek feedback and constructive criticism from colleagues, mentors, clients, and peers to identify areas for improvement, capitalize on strengths, and address blind spots or development opportunities in your professional performance and growth.
- Reflective Practice: Engage in reflective practice by regularly evaluating your actions, decisions, and outcomes, and identifying lessons learned, insights gained, and areas for refinement or adjustment to enhance your effectiveness and impact as an insurance professional.

10.7 Conclusion:
- Recap of key concepts discussed in this chapter.
- Importance of continuous learning and professional development in the insurance industry to stay relevant, competitive, and successful throughout your career.
- Excitement for the journey of lifelong learning, growth, and improvement as you continue to evolve and excel in the dynamic and rewarding field of insurance sales and service.

CONCLUSION

Congratulations on reaching the end of this journey towards becoming a successful insurance producer! Throughout this book, we've explored the essential principles, strategies, and techniques that are foundational to thriving in the dynamic and rewarding field of insurance sales and service. From understanding the fundamentals of the insurance industry to mastering sales techniques, building client relationships, and navigating regulations and compliance, you've gained valuable insights and practical guidance to excel in your role as an insurance professional.

As you reflect on the knowledge and skills you've acquired, remember that success in insurance is not just about closing sales or achieving targets—it's about making a positive impact in the lives of your clients, helping them protect what matters most, and providing peace of mind in times of uncertainty. By approaching your work with integrity, empathy, and a commitment to serving the best interests of your clients, you'll build lasting relationships, earn trust and loyalty, and contribute to the well-being and financial security of individuals, families, and businesses in your community.

As you continue your journey in the insurance industry, embrace a mindset of continuous learning and improvement. Stay curious, stay adaptable, and stay committed to growing your knowledge, honing your skills, and expanding your expertise. Seek out mentorship, seek out opportunities for professional development, and seek out ways to make a difference—not just in your own career, but in the broader landscape of insurance and risk management.

Remember, your journey as an insurance producer is not just about the destination—it's about the experiences you'll have, the challenges you'll overcome, and the relationships you'll build along the way. So, keep striving, keep learning, and keep making a difference. The future of insurance is in your hands, and with dedication, passion, and a relentless pursuit of excellence, the possibilities are limitless.

Thank you for embarking on this journey with us. May your career as an insurance producer be filled with success, fulfillment, and endless opportunities to make a positive impact in the lives of others.

GLOSSARY

1. Insurance: A contract between an individual or entity (the insured) and an insurance company (the insurer), in which the insurer agrees to provide financial protection or reimbursement against specified losses or damages in exchange for payment of a premium.

2. Premium: The amount of money paid by the insured to the insurer in exchange for insurance coverage.

3. Deductible: The amount of money that the insured must pay out of pocket before the insurance coverage kicks in and the insurer starts to pay for covered losses or damages.

4. Coverage Limits: The maximum amount of money that an insurance policy will pay out for covered losses or damages, as specified in the policy contract.

5. Exclusions: Specific events, circumstances, or types of damage that are not covered by an insurance policy, as outlined in the policy contract.

6. Policy Components: The various sections or parts of an insurance policy that outline the terms, conditions, and coverage provided by the policy, including declarations, insuring agreements, conditions, and endorsements.

7. Claims Process: The procedure for filing, processing, and settling insurance claims, including the steps involved, the documentation required, and the roles of the insured, insurer, and claims adjuster.

8. Life Insurance: A type of insurance that provides financial protection to beneficiaries in the event of the insured's death, typically in the form of a lump-sum payment or periodic income payments.

9. Health Insurance: Insurance coverage that pays for medical expenses, including hospitalization, surgery, prescription drugs, and preventive care, incurred by the insured individual or their covered dependents.

10. Property Insurance: Insurance coverage that protects against damage or loss to physical property, such as homes, buildings, vehicles, and personal belongings, caused by covered perils such as fire, theft, or natural disasters.

11. Casualty Insurance: Insurance coverage that provides protection against liability for bodily injury or property damage caused by the insured's actions or negligence, including auto liability, general liability, and professional liability insurance.

12. State Regulations: Laws, rules, and regulations governing the insurance industry at the state level, including licensing requirements, consumer protection provisions, and regulatory oversight by state insurance departments.

13. Ethical Standards: Principles of conduct and professional behavior that govern the actions and decisions of insurance producers, including honesty, integrity, transparency, and a commitment to acting in the best interests of clients.

14. Compliance Practices: Policies, procedures, and practices implemented by insurance producers to ensure adherence to regulatory requirements, industry standards, and ethical guidelines in their business operations and interactions with clients.

15. Customer Relationship Management (CRM) Systems: Software platforms used by insurance producers to organize, manage, and track client interactions, leads, and opportunities, and to facilitate communication and relationship-building with clients.

16. Marketing Automation Tools: Software applications and platforms used to automate marketing activities such as email campaigns, social media posting, and content distribution to attract, engage, and nurture leads and prospects.

17. Needs Assessment: A process for identifying and evaluating clients' insurance needs, goals, and preferences to recommend suitable insurance solutions that meet their specific requirements.

18. Objections: Concerns, hesitations, or objections raised by clients during the sales process regarding the cost, coverage, or suitability of insurance products, which must be addressed and overcome to close the sale successfully.

19. Client Relationships: The connections, interactions, and rapport established between insurance producers and their clients, based on trust, communication, and mutual respect, with the goal of fostering loyalty, satisfaction, and long-term retention.

20. Compliance Management Software: Software tools used by insurance producers to streamline compliance processes, track regulatory requirements, and ensure adherence to industry standards and best practices in their business operations.

21. Professional Designations: Credentials, certifications, and professional designations awarded by insurance associations, industry organizations, and educational institutions to recognize expertise, knowledge, and proficiency in specific areas of insurance specialization.

www.ingramcontent.com/pod-product-compliance
Lightning Source LLC
Chambersburg PA
CBHW050247230526
45470CB00005B/2156